The 'Parents' Time Off' Series

KIDS' NATURE ACTIVITIES

Linda Swainger

Illustrations by
Christine Eddy

Edited by
Cecilia Egan

LEAVES of GOLD
PRESS

First published in 1989 by Egan Publishing Pty Ltd

Revised and updated 2015
Copyright © Leaves of Gold Press 2015

National Library of Australia Cataloguing-in-Publication entry
Creator: Swainger, Linda, author.
Title: Kids' nature activities / Linda Swainger ;
Christine Eddy, illustrator.
Cecilia Egan, editor.

Edition: 2nd edition
ISBN: 9781925110760 (paperback)
Series: Parents' time off series ; 9.

Target Audience: For primary school age (6-12 year old)
Subjects: Nature craft--Juvenile literature.
Handicraft for children.

Other Creators/Contributors: Eddy, Christine, illustrator.

Dewey Number: 745.925
ABN 67 099 575 078

LEAVES of GOLD PRESS

ABN 67 099 575 078

PO Box 9113, Brighton, 3186, Victoria, Australia
www.leavesofgoldpress.com

CONTENTS

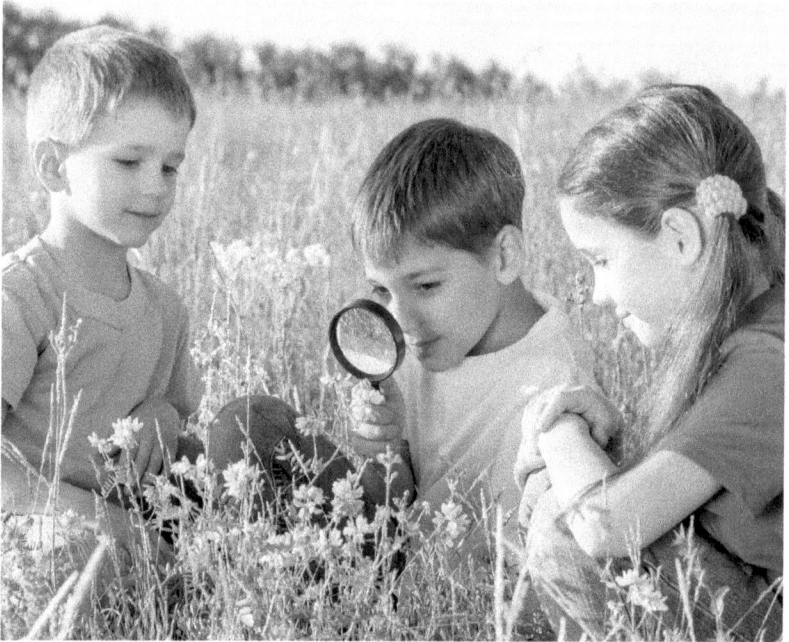

INTRODUCTION

The activities in this fascinating book use materials that are easily found in the garden, at the beach, in the bush or at the park.

Children of all ages will have hours of fun making decorative and useful items out of seedpods, seashells and other natural objects.

FUN AND DECORATION

Dyeing Grasses
Dyeing Flowers
Jungle Woven Wall Hanging
Creeper Weaving
Need Some Water?
Leaf Skeletons
Coloured Sand Paperweight
Nature Prints
Nature Rubbings
Natural Dyes
Pressed Flowers and Leaves

DYEING GRASSES

Materials:
- Dried grasses (ie with furry heads)
- Newspapers
- Food dyes, or edicole dyes
- Rubber gloves
- Wooden spoon and old ice-cream container (or other plastic one)
- Jar or vase
- Water

Instructions:
1. Spread the newspapers thickly on the surface on which you will be working.
2. Put on the rubber gloves and mix the dye with some warm water in the icecream container.
3. Take a handful of the dried grasses and lie them in the dye in the icecream container.
4. Use the wooden spoon to move them around and keep them immersed in the water.
5. When the grasses have turned a dark colour take them out and spread them on the newspaper until most of the water is absorbed and then stand them in a vase to dry.
- If you use a hair dryer to dry the dyed grasses they will fluff up nicely.
- You can use dyed grasses in dried arrangements.

DYEING FLOWERS

Materials:
- Clear jar (ie coffee jar or clear vase)
- Food dyes, or edicole dyes
- Flowers, ie carnations, lilies, daffo-
  dils - or try some from your garden.
- Water

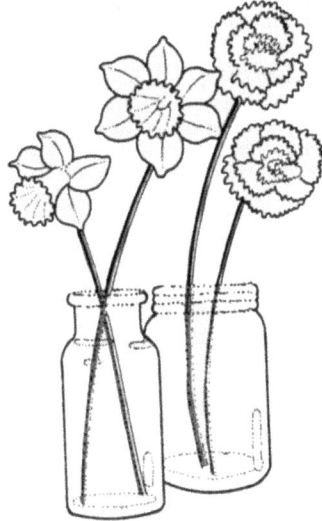

Instructions:
1. Choose the flowers you wish to dye. Some change colour quickly and
   some more slowly. With a few types of flowers the dyes seem to kill
   then sooner than they change colour. Try a few different kinds and
   compare the results and time it takes to change colour.
2. Put a few drops of the dye into the jar or water and insert the flowers
   you wish to dye.
3. Watch for a couple of days as the dye creeps up the stems and into
   the flower.

Variation:
- When your flowers have changed colour, why not press them and use
  them for bookmarks or in a frame?
- The more dye you put in the darker the flowers will turn.

JUNGLE WOVEN WALL HANGING

Materials:
- Two strong sticks - the same length
- One ball of wool or string
- Lots of long, natural objects, ie twigs, grasses, flower stems, long leaves, etc
- Scissors

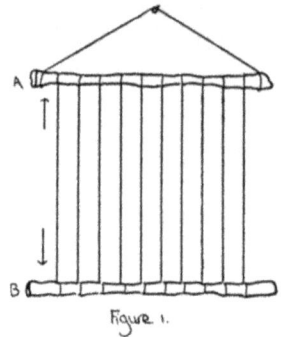

Figure 1.

Method:
1. Decide how long you would like to have your wall hanging. This will also depend on how much natural 'stuff' you have to weave onto it.
2. Make your weaving base by tying lengths of wool in between the sticks at the same distance apart and length from stick A to stick B (Figure 1).
3. Weave the collected items through your weaving base using "over then under" fashion.

CREEPER WEAVING

Materials:
- *String*
- *Two strong sticks the same length*
- *A potted creeper ie. ivy, jasmine or some other quick growing species*

Method:
1. Try to get a potted creeper as long as you can so you can start the weaving straight away.
2. Make your weaving base by tying lengths of the string in between the sticks at the same distance apart and the same length.
3. As your creeper grows thread it in woven fashion over and under the weaving base. Make sure you keep the creeper watered so it keeps growing.

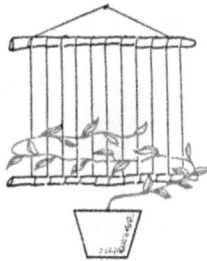

Variation:
- Buy a commercial creeper grower to weave your creeper through - ie. one that is inserted into the pot the creeper is planted in.
- Have two different types of creeper growing through your weaving base at the same time. This looks very interesting.

NEED SOME WATER?

Collect Your Own!

Method1:

Materials:
- *Plant with low branches*
- *Large glass jar*

Method:
1. Place the glass jar over one branch of the plant on an angle. Prop it up with soil or stones, if necessary.
2. Leave the jar there overnight and then see if much water is in the jar.

Using this method:
How much can you collect overnight?
How much could you collect in a week?
How many days will it take to get a cup full?

Method 2:

Materials:
- *Spade*
- *An empty tin*
- *Stone*
- *Leaves*
- *Plastic*

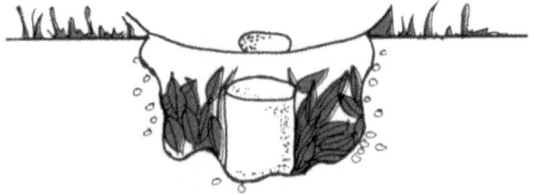

Method:
1. Dig a hole and fill it with fresh plants and leaves.
2. Put the tin in the middle of the hole.
3. Cover the hole with a sheet of plastic and put a stone on top - directly above the tin.
4. Leave overnight and see how much you've collected.

Which method is quickest?

LEAF SKELETONS

You must ask an adult to help with heating the water.

Materials:
- One large pot
- One dish brush or nail brush
- Newspaper
- Collection of different types of leaves
- Washing soda
- Water
- Stove
- Plastic container, ie icecream
- Bleach
- Sieve

Instructions:
1. Half fill your pot with water mixed with a handful of washing soda and heat it until it is almost boiling.
2. Carefully drop the leaves into the water and turn the heat down to simmer them for one hour (or until the fleshy part comes away from the leaf skeleton).
3. Slowly pour the water out of the pot using a sieve.
4. Spread the leaves onto the newspaper and let them cool.
5. Use the dishbrush to gently brush away the fleshy parts of the leaves.
6. In your plastic container mix some water with one teaspoon of bleach.
7. Put the leaf skeletons into the bleach mixture and leave for one hour.
8. Slowly pour the bleach mixture out using the sieve to catch the leaf skeletons.
9. Leave the skeletons in the sieve and rinse under a gentle cold tap.

COLOURED SAND PAPERWEIGHT

Materials:
- Glass jar with lid
- Dry sand - enough to fill the jar
- Food colouring
- Large trays
- Freezer bags
- Plastic or paper funnel

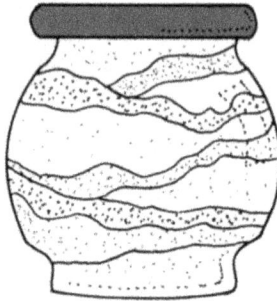

Instructions:
1. Divide the sand into portions. Leave one portion natural and dye the other portions different colours by placing handfuls into a freezer bag with a few drops of food colouring. Shake the bag to mix the colour, then spread the sand on a tray to dry. (You can put it in an oven on low heat).
2. Make a paper funnel by twisting a sheet of paper into a cone with a small hole at one end and fastening it with sticky tape, or use a plastic funnel. Put the funnel into the jar and pour one colour of sand into it, making waves and slopes.
3. Use alternating colours to build up a pattern until the jar is full to the brim, then screw the lid on tightly.

NATURE PRINTS

Materials:
- Natural objects collected from the garden, ie leaves, grasses, flowers, twigs, stones, etc.
- Paint
- Paint brush or roller
- Newspaper
- Sheets of absorbent paper, ie white butcher's paper

Method:
1. Spread out some newspaper on a table and put the butcher's paper on top.
2. Paint onto the natural objects and place them paint side down on the butcher's paper.
3. Place newspaper over the top and press down gently to make an impression.
4. Carefully remove the natural objects and see the print they've left.

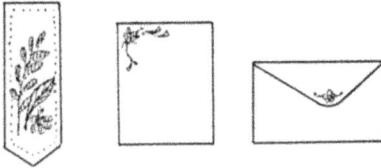

Variations:
- Use this activity to make gift wrap and cards for special occasions. Cover printed bookmarks with clear plastic or spray with varnish.

- Use shells, seaweeds and other beach found items for a different effect.

NATURE RUBBINGS

Materials:
- Thick crayons
- White or plain coloured paper, ie butcher's or computer.
- Collection of natural items from your garden

Method:
1. Arrange the collected natural objects the way you would like them to appear on the finished product. Stick them down firmly, eg with Blu-tack.
2. Cover them with the sheet of paper and hold it firmly with one hand or stick it down.
3. Now gently rub with the crayon on its side over each object.

These look much better if the whole page is covered in colour and not just sections near the natural objects.

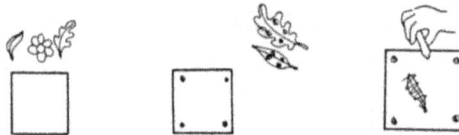

Variations:
- Use all leaves - or all twigs on each sheet and compare how different or similar types of the one thing can be.
- Use this activity to make gift wrap, bookmarks and greeting cards for special occasions.

- Use shells or other beach things.

NATURAL DYES

You can tie-dye your clothes or dye Easter eggs using plants!
Ask an adult to help you with the boiling water.

Plants you can use:
- *Onion skins (these are quickest)*
- *Gum leaves*
- *Bark*
- *The green husks of walnuts and walnut leaves nylon won't take*

Fabrics you can use:
- *Wool*
- *Silk*
- *Cotton*
- *Linen (synthetics such as natural dyes)*

- ***You can only dye light coloured clothes.***

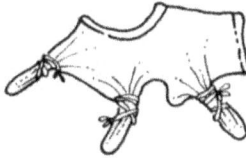

Other Materials:
- *A big old saucepan*
- *A long-handled spoon for stirring*
- *A mesh bag such as an orange bag or a bag made out of pantyhose*

Onion Skins:
These give a yellow colour.

Place the brown outer skins of three brown onions in a mesh bag, tie up the bag and put it in the old saucepan with plenty of water. Boil for half an hour, add the piece of clothing and simmer for thirty to forty-five minutes. For eggs simmer only five minutes.

Gum Leaves:
These give rusty reds, or yellows or tans. Different varieties of gum leaves give different colours.

Bark:
This gives a lemon colour. Try different sorts of bark, but soak it overnight in water first.

Green husks of walnuts and walnut leaves:
These give a brown colour.

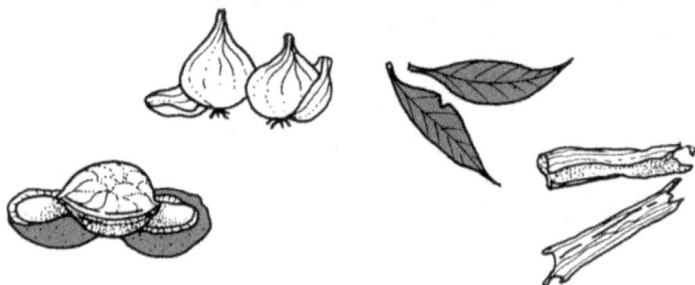

Instructions:
For gum leaves, bark and green walnut husks, tie a handful of the plant in a mesh bag, boil for one hour in plenty of water, add clothing and simmer for two hours.

Tie-dyeing:
To make dyed patterns on clothing make little bunches in it and tie them tightly with string or elastic bands before dyeing.

To make dyed patterns on eggs tie them up in cloth before dyeing.

Variations:
Try dyeing with geranium petals, geranium leaves or dahlia heads.

PRESSED FLOWERS AND LEAVES

Collect small flowers and thin decorative leaves such as fern leaves from your garden. Pick them on a day when it hasn't rained - the less moisture there is, the quicker they will dry.

Fold the plants between two sheets of absorbent paper then put the papers flat under a heavy weight. A pile of books is good for pressing flowers. The plants will take three or four days to dry, sometimes longer.

Use pressed flowers and leaves to make your own bookmarks, note-paper, envelopes, greeting cards and flower pictures.

SEEDPODS AND GUMNUTS

DECORATED MAGNETS

Materials:
- *Heavy card or leather*
- *Magnets (available from craft stores)*
- *Spray varnish*
- *Strong Glue*
- *Natural materials - ie gumnuts, seeds, grasses, ferns, bark pieces, feathers, dried flowers or leaves, pressed flowers, etc.*

Instructions:
1. Decide what size and shape you would like your magnet to be and cut this from the card or leather.
2. Arrange your natural materials in an appropriate design beside your magnet shape.
3. Apply plenty of strong glue to the card or leather and transfer your natural materials in your design to the card or leather, pressing down firmly into the glue.
4. When the glue is dry spray with two to three coats of clear varnish.
5. When the varnish is dry, turn over your magnet top and place a large dab of glue onto the non-magnetic side of your magnet and stick it on the back of the card or leather.

- These make great gifts, or use them to hold notes to your fridge.

CHRISTMAS WREATH

Materials:
- *Lots of creeper such as wisteria or else long strands from a willow tree, stripped of leaves.*
- *Sprays of seedpods on twigs, such as ti-tree, gumnuts, casuarina (sheoak)*
- *Dried grasses and leaves*
- *Spray varnish*
- *Pretty ribbon*

Instructions:
1. Reserve one or two very long creepers.
2. Divide the bunch of creepers in half, form each half into a circle, form a wreath and then mingle them together so that the end of one circle is in the middle of the other. This adds strength.
3. Tightly bind the very long creepers all around the outside of the wreath, then tuck the ends under.
4. Poke in the seedpods, leaves, grasses, etc. close together around the wreath then spray on clear varnish.
5. Add a pretty ribbon tied in a bow and hang it up.

Note: When the creepers have dried they will hold their shape. If they start to come apart before that, bind them with sticky tape.

SEEDPOD CHRISTMAS ORNAMENTS

Materials:
- Any hard seedpods, such as banksia, casuarina, gumnuts, ti-tree, acorns.
- Gold or silver paint
- Gold, silver, green or red cotton for hanging
- Tiny wire rings (available from hardware or haberdashery, or make your own by twisting wire around a pencil). Bent open paper clips or hooks from hook- and-eye sets can be used, or buy jewellery clasps from your craft shop.
- Silicon glue

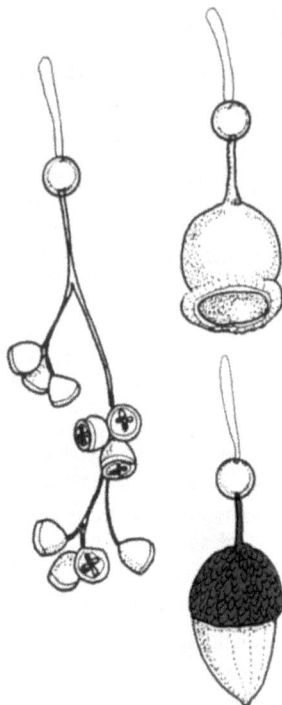

Instructions:
1. Spread newspaper on your working surface and paint the seedpods gold or silver. Allow to dry.
2. Use the silicon glue to attach the wire rings to one end of each seedpod. Allow to dry.
3. Thread the cotton through the ring, make a loop and knot it together. Your ornament is now ready to hang on the Christmas Tree.

TABLE CENTREPIECES

An adult may have to help with the cutting

Materials:
- *Plasticine*
- *Heavy Card*
- *Strong Glue*
- *Spray Varnish*
- *Natural Objects, ie gumnuts, twigs, leaves, pine cones, nuts, seed pods, pebbles, etc.*

Instructions:

These centrepieces can take on any shape or form you like. They may be on a circle, a wreath shape, triangular, square, etc. It all depends on what shape and size you cut your heavy card.

1. Ask an adult to cut out your thick card to the desired size and shape.
2. Cover the card with a layer of strong glue and then spread the plasticine in a layer on top of the glue.
3. Stick the natural objects into the plasticine firmly.
4. Spray with two or three coats of spray varnish.

Variations:
- To make a wreath use a large and a small plate to draw this on the card, then cut it out and stick on lots of natural objects using plenty of glue. Varnish when dry.
- For the dinner table stick a couple of candles into the plasticine.
- For a different effect, spray the centrepiece with a coloured spray paint or gold or silver.

PLASTER NATURE CASTS: IMPRESSIONS

With impressions, the objects are removed from the plaster, and their shape remains.

Materials:
- *Any natural object, eg shells, twigs, leaves, seedpods or gumnuts*
- *Bag of casting plaster (Hardware Stores)*
- *Empty icecream conntainer - large*
- *Jug of water*
- *Old spoon - as you won't be able to use it in the kitchen again*
- *Shallow container the size and shape you wish your impressions to turn out, eg foil, pie dish, paper plate, foil patty pans, margarine container.*

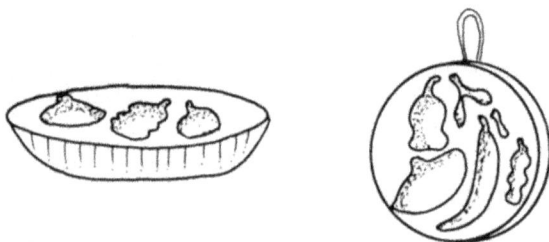

Instructions:
You will need to be quick at making this, as the plaster sets very quickly!
1. Gather together the natural materials you wish to use.
2. Mix the casting plaster to the directions on the packet. Stir quickly until it forms a thick paste.
3. Pour the plaster into the mould you will be using, eg foil pie plate.
4. Make a print with each natural object, pressing it down firmly into the plaster then taking it away.
5. Leave the cast overnight to dry thoroughly then peel the pie plate off the back.

PLASTER NATURE CASTS: INSETS

With insets the objects remain embedded in the plaster.

To make insets, follow the instructions for Plaster Nature Casts: Impressions. However, instead of Steps 3 and 4 do this:

Pour the mixture into the dish you wish to use and then insert the natural objects so that part of each is embedded in the plaster and part sticking out

Or

Place the objects into the dish and then pour the plaster over so that each is covered in plaster but still recognizable in form.

Continue with Step 5 as for "Impressions".

• Use these casts as paperweights or embed a candle in the middle for a candleholder.

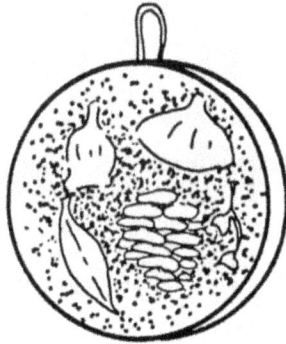

Variations:
• Attach a hook to make a wall hanging by bending a paper clip open and placing this in the dish before pouring in the plaster. When the mould is dry one end of the paper clip (the exposed one) can be carved out to form a hook.
• Make an impression of your hand.
• Make coloured plaster by adding powder paint to the dry plaster or by adding food dye to the water.

NATURE PICTURE FRAMES

You must ask an adult to help with the cutting

Basic Frame:

Materials:
- Sheet of firm cardboard
- Ruler
- Pencil
- Sharp scissors or Stanley type knife

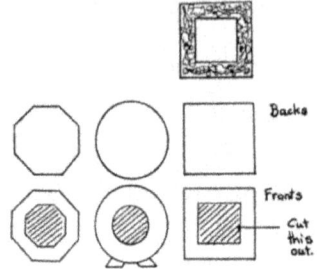

Instructions:
1. Decide what shape you wish to use and draw two identical ones on the thick cardboard. Ask an adult to cut these out.
2. On one piece of this draw a smaller shape. This will form the front part. The picture fits in behind (see above)
3. Have an adult cut away the section drawn in.
4. Put a line of glue around the outside edge of the back section - leaving one side free to slide the picture in.
5. Set the front section on top of the back section and press firmly.
6. Insert photo or other picture into the frame through the open edge.

Variations:
- Use coloured cardboard or cover it with wrapping paper so it will be attractive where there are no natural objects.
- Instead of inserting a photograph why not press some flowers, fix them onto cardboard and insert.

Nature Frame:
- Make the frame as above up to Step 3 - use strong glue to paste on natural objects, gumnuts, dried grasses, leaves, pressed flowers, small pebbles, feathers, shells, etc.
- When the glue is dry spray the front section with two to three coats of clear varnish, then complete the frame as per above 'basic frame recipe'

SHELLS AND PEBBLES

Shell Jewel Box
Shell Plant Pot
Stone Mice
Rock Animals

SHELL JEWEL BOXES

Materials:
- Assorted shells collected from the beach.
- Strong glue
- Pencil
- One box with lid available from craft shops. Both cardboard and wood are suitable.
- Spray varnish

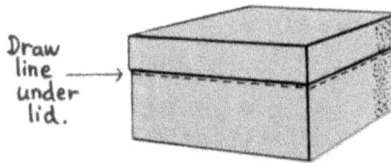

Draw line under lid. ——→

Instructions:
1. Using the pencil, draw a faint line under the bottom lip of the box's lid where it meets the box. This forms the top of where shells will be attached so the lid may still fit neatly on.
2. Arrange the shells on the lid of the box in the desired pattern.
3. When you have the design you wish, apply lots of glue to the lid and paste the shells in place.
4. Repeat steps two and three on the other surfaces of the box (except the underneath and above the pencil line).
5. When the glue is dry, spray the finished product with two to three coats of spray varnish. Put some cotton wool in the bottom and it's ready for your jewels.

SHELL PLANT POT

Materials:
- Ordinary plastic plant pot (available from department stores and nurseries).
- Shells, pebbles or both.
- Strong glue, such as silicon glue.
- Varnish

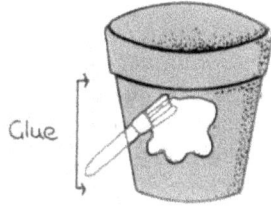

Glue

Instructions:
1. Wash and dry your plant pot
2. Coat the pot with strong glue around the outside up to the rim
3. Press the shells or glue pebbles onto the pot in any pattern you wish.
4. When glue is dry give two to three coats of varnish for a shiny finish.

STONE MICE

Materials:
- *Small piece of soft leather or stiff fabric*
- *Strong glue*
- *Round shaped pebble*
- *Paints*
- *Three pipe cleaners each one 6 cm in length*
- *Spray varnish*

Figure 1.

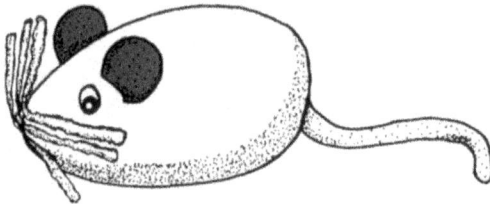

Instructions:
1. Clean the pebble with soapy water and a bristle brush (ie nail brush). Dry thoroughly and spray with varnish.
2. Cut out two ear shapes from the leather (figure 1) and a long strip for the tail.
2. Stick the ears and tail into place on the pebble using the strong glue.
3. Use the paints to paint two eyes on the pebble.
4. Fold the pipe cleaners in half and use the glue to attach the middle (folded) section of the pipe cleaners to the pebble to form whiskers.

Variation:
- You can also use plastic eyes bought from craft stores for a more 'real' looking mouse.

ROCK ANIMALS

Materials:
* *Collection of small rocks*
* *Strong glue*
* *Movable eyes (available from craft stores)*
* *Spray varnish*

Instructions:
1. Look carefully at the shaped stones you have. Do any look like ears, legs, heads or bodies?
2. Arrange your stones into an animal or person, using larger ones for bodies, a little smaller for heads and small ones for ears, tails, feet, etc.
3. When you have your figure looking as desired use the strong glue to paste it together. Paste on the eyes.
4. When the paste is dry, spray your figure with varnish for a nice shiny finish.

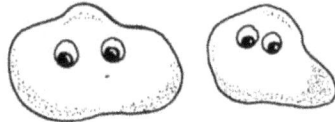

Note: Before you varnish the animal, you might like to paint it with stripes, spots, etc.

Variations:
* Pet rocks - simply glue eyes on to a varnished pebble.
* You can use felt to make noses, mouths or punk hair.
* Rock Group or Family - put some plasticine in the bottom of a dish and push several pet rocks into it so that they sit firmly in place.
* Use potting mix and grass seed instead of plasticine to grow a "jungle" for your family.

INSECTS, LITTLE BEASTS AND BIRDS

BIRD FEEDERS

Foil Plate Feeder:

Materials:
- String
- Sharp knife
- Foil pie plate or bowl

Method:
1. Using the sharp knife make four small holes in the sides of the pie plate (figure 1).
2. Attach string pieces of the same length into each hole and knot them together above the plate (figure 2).

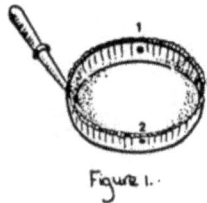

Now it's ready to fill and hang.

CARTON FEEDER:

Materials:
- Scissors
- Empty milk carton
- Pen
- String

Method:
1. Cut away a portion from the centre of the milk carton on three sides.
2. Make a hole in the top of the milk carton and attach some string
3. Fill and hang.

Foil Plate Feeder.

Carton Feeder.

Figure 1.

Figure 2.

Carton feeder

FRUIT BAG BIRD FEEDER

Materials:
- Mesh fruit bag (ie orange bag)
- Mixture of fat, bacon rind, bread crumbs, sultanas, peanut butter
- String

Instructions:
1. Fill the bag with the food mixture and hang it from a high tree branch.

PINE CONE BIRD FEEDER

Materials:
- Large pine cone
- String
- Breadcrumbs, bird seed, peanut butter, fat, sultanas

Instructions:
1. Tie the piece of string to the large end of the pine cone.
2. Roll the pine cone in the peanut butter and fat and then roll in the breadcrumbs, bird seed and/or sultanas.
3. Hang the pine cone from a high tree branch.

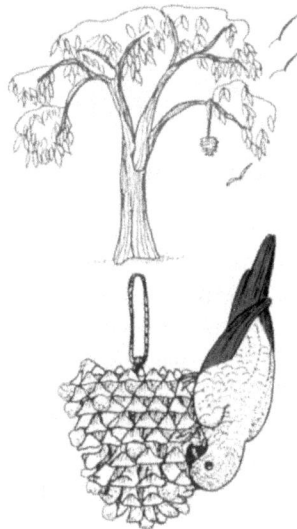

COLLECTING LITTLE BEASTS

What to Look For:

- Butterflies
- Ants
- Moths
- Flies
- Dragon flies
- Water beetles

- Grasshoppers
- Crickets
- Caterpillars
- Centipedes
- Ladybirds
- Beetles

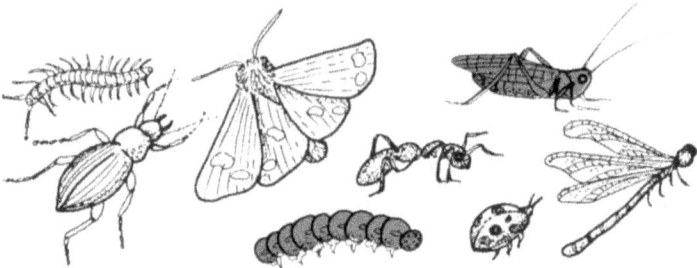

Don't forget to return the beasts to where you found them after you've had a good look.

Why?

Because little beasts need to live in their homes, just like we do. And they are an important part of nature. We should respect and care for all living things, no matter how tiny they are!

Where to Look:

- In the air
- In the water
- Under stones, pebbles, rocks
- In and around bushes
- Under things that have been lying around for a while, ie tyres, bricks.
- Around flowers and fruit trees.

HOW TO CATCH SOME LITTLE BEASTS:

Plastic Bug Catchers
These are available from most department and toy stores. They are specifically designed for catching and having a close look at insects and allowing them a good air supply. They come with instructions for use.

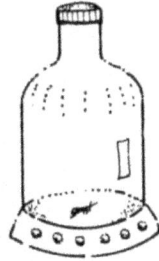

Jar Bug Catchers
These can be empty plastic or glass jars with lids. Holes can be punched in the lid for ventilation using a hammer and nail, or you can cover the jar top with clear plastic food wrap and jab holes in it with a skewer. It can be fastened on with an elastic band.

Paper Collection
Get a large sheet of white paper (ie butcher's paper) or a white bedsheet. Carefully place it under a large bush. Get an old newspaper and roll it up. Use the rolled up newspaper to hit the bush sharply two or three times above the white paper. Have a look and see what insects have dropped down. Pop them into a container with a lid for a longer viewing time or a closer look.

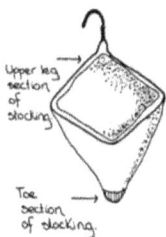

Stocking Insect Net
To make one of these you will need the leg of a stocking and a wire coat hanger. First you will need to bend the coat hanger into a diamond shape and then after cutting the stocking to approx 50 cm from the toe, stretch the cut end over the coat hanger frame. This can be fastened in place by either sewing it down or holding it together with pins.

WORMERY

Materials:
- One large glass container, eg small fish tank.
- Four to six worms
- Garden soil containing leaf litter
- Water
- Lettuce leaves or fresh garden leaves
- Black paper
- Sticky tape

Instructions:
1. To collect worms try watering a garden bed or around vegetables or compost piles, and then digging in the moist earth.
2. Collect some garden soil and put it into your glass tank. Fill it up almost to the top. (You may need to put it in place first as the tank with dirt in it will be very heavy).
3. Finally chop up a lettuce leaf and some fresh leaves, and mix this with the soil. Also mix in some dead bugs and flies if you can find any.

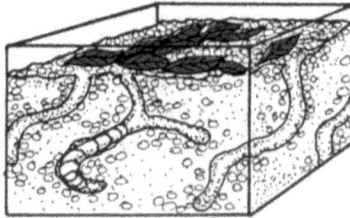

4. Put your worms into their new home and cover around the four sides with the black paper so that it is dark all around. (Don't worry about covering the top). Put some fresh leaves on top of the soil.
5. Keep the soil moist but not wet and in three or four days undo one side of the black paper and you will see some worm tunnels against the glass.
* Don't forget to let the worms go back into the garden when you have had a good look.

ANT FARM [Formicarium]

Materials:
- One wooden seed tray approximately 40 cm x 30 cm (available from a plant nursery)
- Sheet of plastic
- Plaster of paris (from craft or hardware shops)
- Spoon and plastic blowl (eg. ice cream container)
- Ants
- Small dish of honey
- Small piece of wood 8 cm deep x 26 cm long.
- Soil
- Wood glue
- Piece of glass 30 cm x 30 cm
- Piece of glass 30 cm x 10 cm.

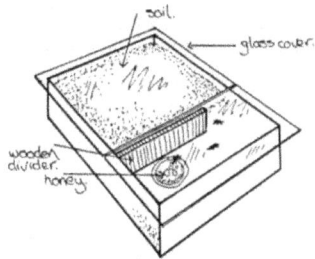

Note: To catch ants leave a piece of food such as meat or honey, outside. In a few hours ants will find it. If you want a Queen Ant, which is bigger, with wings, you will have to dig up an ant's nest.

Instructions:
1. Lay the sheet of plastic along the bottom and sides of the wooden tray.
2. Mix up the plaster of paris as per the directions on the packet. Pour the mixture into the tray to within 3 cm of the top.
3. Lay the 8 cm x 26 cm piece of wood 10 cm from one end of the tray pushing it into the plaster so the top is level with the top of the wooden tray. Ants will pass back and forth through the space at the end of this "wall".
4. When the plaster is dry fill the larger area with soil.
5. Paste a line of wood glue around the outer perimeter of the larger area of the container and set the 30 x 30 cm piece of glass on top. This forms the nest area.
6. Cover the smaller area with the smaller piece of glass. Don't paste this down as it needs to be removable. This forms the feeding area and entrance to the nest.
7. Place the ants in the nest entrance with the dish of honey.

KEEPING TADPOLES

To keep tadpoles long enough for them to turn into frogs you will need to be very patient as this process can take around three months. It can also become very smelly if you don't look after them carefully (it can be a bit smelly anyway after a few weeks).

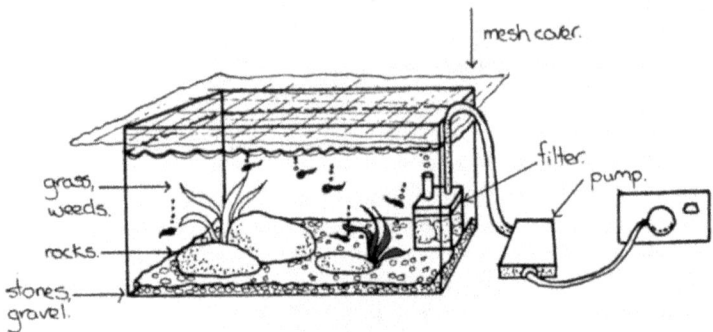

There are many ways to keep tadpoles. I have found the best way, the least smelly and easiest to see changes occurring is with the use of a small fish tank and aquarium filter. This method is a lot less trouble to look after also. If a tank and filter are unavailable you can use a large bowl and plenty of changes of fresh weed and grass to keep a high oxygen content in the water. Whichever method you use you will also need a fine mesh (plastic or wire) netting cover for the top so that when you do eventually get frogs they won't jump out before you get a good look at them.

KEEPING TADPOLES (Continued)

Set your bowl or tank up as for the setting up of the aquarium, (see previous page), using a bit of water from the river or pond where the tadpoles came from as well as clean water. Rain water is best for them as it doesn't contain the additives that tap water has.

Finding the tadpoles can be a slow process. You can use your hand however it is best to make a stocking insect net (see index) as they won't slide away when you eventually find them.

Tadpoles like to live and hide amongst the gravel, grasses and litter of the bottom of rivers and ponds and will also prefer the bottom of your tadpole tank. This is the place to look for them. They tend to be more predominant over the spring and summer months but can often be found all year through.

After catching your tadpoles transfer them with some of their own pond water into your tank. Try to remove much of the litter you may have also collected so that the tank water doesn't become too polluted.

Put the mesh cover on the tank and regularly change the weed or grass. You don't have to feed tadpoles as long as you keep living waterweed with them, but frogs will need live flies and spiders.

NATURAL
JEWELLERY

Gumnut Bracelet and Necklace
Shell Bracelet and Necklace
Disk Brooch
Seedpod Brooch

GUMNUT NECKLACE
AND BRACELET

Materials:
- Jewellery clasps and natural coloured beads from craft shops
- Thin leather string or other strong string
- Small gumnuts (approximately 1 cm in size)
- Spray varnish (gloss)
- 60 cm thin leather string for necklace
- Silicon glue or other strong glue

Instructions:
1. Spray the gumnuts with two or three coats of clear varnish. Allow to dry.
2. Open out the jewellery clasps enough for them to grip the stalk of each gumnut, and glue them on. Some clasps need an additional ring (from craft shops) for the string to pass through.
3. For the bracelet measure a piece of leather string long enough to go around your wrist comfortably with enough left to tie.
4. Make a knot approximately 2 cm from one end of the leather string and string on your breads and gumnuts, either alternately or in a pattern.
5. When you are within 2 cm of the other end knot the leather string to hold the beads in place.
6. Ask someone to help you tie your bracelet to your wrist.

Variation:
- Try using a variety of seedpods.

SHELL NECKLACE AND BRACELET

Materials:
- *Assorted small shells*
- *Jewellery clasps from craft shops*
- *Clear, glossy spray varnish*
- *Leather strip long enough for a necklace or bracelet to fit you*
- *Silicon glue or other strong glue*

Instructions:
1. Wash and dry shells. Measure length of leather strip to desired length for your necklace or bracelet ie 90 cm for necklace or 30 cm for bracelet.
2. Spray the shells with clear, glossy varnish. Allow to dry.
3. Open out the jewellery clasps until the flat part will sit against the shell leaving the loop sticking up to be threaded. Glue on, and allow to dry.
4. Thread each shell onto the leather string. Tie around neck or wrist.

Variations:
- Purchase some beads or dye some macaroni in food dye and thread on a shell and a piece of macaroni then another shell - or make a pattern in your threading.

- **Note:** Some beach-found shells already have holes in them for threading!

DISK BROOCH

Note: You should ask an adult to do the cutting.

Materials:
- *Natural objects - or - an assortment of seeds*
- *Heavy cardboard*
- *Sharp, Stanley type knife*
- *Pencil*
- *Safety pin or clasp available from craft stores*
- *Strong glue*
- *Spray varnish*

Instructions:
1. Draw or trace a circle (or another shape you may wish your brooch to be) onto the heavy card. Ask an adult to cut this out with the sharp knife.
2. Use plenty of glue and stick your seeds or natural objects in an attractive arrangement on one side of the brooch.
3. When glue is dry spray the arrangement with two to three coats of clear varnish
4. When the varnish is dry turn the brooch over and attach the pin or clasp to the centre using a large dob of strong glue.

Variation:
- If you find a dead beetle you could glue this on to your disk and varnish it, for a "Beetle Brooch".

SEEDPOD BROOCH

Materials:

- Gum leaves
- Small seed pods in a cluster on a stem, such as gumnuts or ti-tree pods.
- Florists wire or fine fuse wire
- Safety pin or brooch clasp available from craft shops
- Spray varnish

Instructions:

1. Join the leaves and gum nuts together in an attractive cluster with the fuse wire. Bind tightly.
2. Attach the safety pin or clasp to the back of the brooch under the cluster so it is disguised, by tightly binding fuse wire around it.
3. Spray with two to three coats of clear varnish.

MINIATURE AND BOTTLE GARDENS

BOTTLE GARDENS

Any type of bottle is suitable as long as the neck is wide enough for small plants to fit through.

Containers with lids:
When using a sealed container condensation often clouds the glass. Whenever this happens ventilate the container by removing the lid or stopper for a few days.

Suitable small plants for Miniature or Bottle Gardens:
Ivy, Ferns, African Violets, Pepperomia varieties, Prayer plants, Pilea (Aluminium plants) Miniature Palms, Zebra plants.

MAKING A GARDEN IN A NARROW-NECKED BOTTLE

- Use paper to make a funnel for the insertion of soil and plants into the right places. Or use a cardboard cylinder ie from a roll of paper towel.

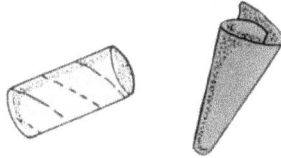

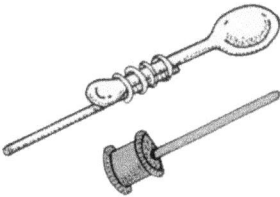

- To make a hole for planting the plants use a spoon tied to a piece of stick. This acts as a spade.

- To press down the soil use a wooden cotton spool attached to a stick.

- To clean the inside glass of the bottle tie some sponge to a stick.
- Use two long sticks as tongs to insert plants and shapely stones.

- To make your bottle garden use the same procedure as for the Soft Drink Bottle Garden.

SHELL GARDENS

Materials:

- A variety of shells as large as possible
- Spray varnish
- Plaster or plasticine
- Small dish eg a foil pie plate
- Small seeds eg cress, mustard, grass

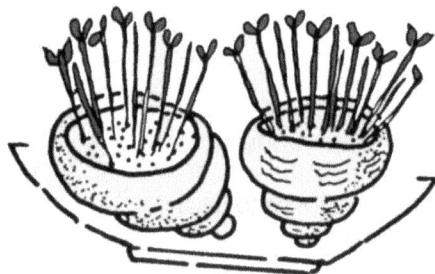

Instructions:

1. Wash the shells carefully and leave to dry on some newspaper.
2. When dry spray the outsides of the shells with the varnish.
3. Put the plaster or plasticine into the bottom of the small dish and insert the dry shells into the dish with the open end of the shell easily accessible.
4. Put some soil into each shell and plant the seeds into them.
5. Water regularly and watch your garden grow.

MINIATURE LANDSCAPE

Materials:

- A shallow plant container such as a bonsai pot or large terracotta saucer
- Pebbles and charcoal for drainage
- Potting mix
- Moss and tiny plants
- Small flat pebbles for paths
- A mirror for a lake
- Little figurines, houses and bridges made of plastic or

Instructions:

1. Place a layer of charcoal and pebbles in the dish, followed by a layer of moist potting mix.
2. Create hills and valleys in the soil.
3. Put in the tiny plants for trees and cover everything else with moss for grass. Water lightly and then add the mirror lake.
4. Add pebble pathways, figurines and houses.
5. Put your miniature landscape in a light place and keep it watered.

- You can make your own houses with glue and matchsticks.
- It is fun to move the figurines around and make up stories about them.

SOFT DRINK BOTTLE GARDEN

Note: An adult will have to help with the cutting.

Materials:
- *Two litre plastic bottle*
- *Sharp knife (ie Stanley type)*
- *Potting mixture*
- *Small plants*
- *Charcoal (necessary for drainage)*
- *Pebbles*
- *Shapely stones*

Instructions:
1. Wash the bottle well and soak it in warm water to remove the label and black bottom section, which you keep.
2. Ask an adult to use the sharp knife to carefully cut off the top section of the bottle from where it starts to taper in at the neck.
3. Place a thin layer of pebbles in the bottom of the black section of the bottle.
4. Place a layer of charcoal on top of the pebbles and then some potting mix on top. Fill the black section to the top.
5. Make a small dent in the soil and insert the plants where desired. Place the stones where you wish and pat down the soil.
6. Spray the garden with water and cover with the upturned clear portion of the bottle.

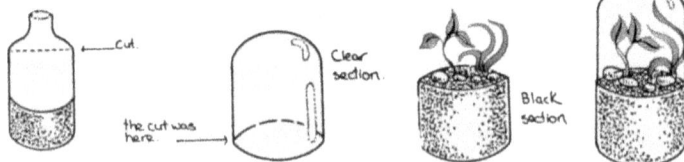

WATER GARDEN

Materials:
- Sand
- Freshwater plants (available from pet shops or aquariums)
- Large glass jar
- A few large shells
- Sheet of paper
- Scissors
- Small pebbles

Instructions:
1. Wash and dry the glass jar and shells thoroughly.
2. Pour two to three centimeters of sand into the bottom of the jar.
3. Fill each shell with sand and arrange them on the bottom of the jar facing upwards.
4. Cut the paper into a circle that will fit on the top of the sand and shells in the jar.
5. Place the paper into the jar, flatten it down and gently trickle water into the jar. When the jar is full remove the paper circle. This method stops the water from disturbing the sand.
6. Put a freshwater plant into each shell so that the roots are embedded in the sand.
7. Keep the jar full of water and put in a sunny place.

GROWING THINGS

HAIRY HARRY

Materials:
- Old stocking leg
- Grass seed
- Potting mix
- Yoghurt container (small) or paper cup.
- Water

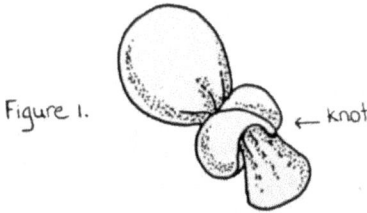

Figure 1.   ← knot

Method:
1. Mix some potting mix with a sprinkle of grass seeds.
2. Cut the leg of the stocking so that you have a length from the toe up of approximately 20 cm.
3. Fill the toe of the stocking with the dirt/grass seed mix. When it is about the size of a tennis ball, tie the stocking. (See Figure 1)
4. Put some water in the bottom of the yoghurt container. Wet the dirt ball and sit it on the yoghurt container so the loose part of the stocking is in the water.
5. Water regularly and grass will soon grow like green hair. If you want to add features, cut them out of felt or paper and stick them on with a sewing pin.

Variations:
- Make a few, vary the sizes and have a "hairy family"
- Decorate the bottom of the yoghurt containers with fabric and materials etc. to make them look like clothes
- Give Harry and his friends some weird hairdos.

FUZZY CATERPILLARS

Materials:
- Old stocking leg
- Polystyrene meat tray
- Potting mix
- Grass seed
- Water

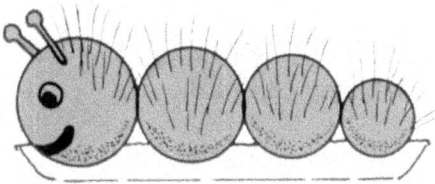

Method:
1. Mix some potting mix with a sprinkle of grass seeds.
2. Fill the toe of the stocking with the dirt/grass mix until you have a rounded end.
3. Tie a knot firmly holding the dirt mix in a ball.
4. Put more dirt/seed mix in the stocking until you have another ball shape and tie again.
5. Continue repeating step four until your caterpillar is the desired length.
6. Put water in the polystyrene tray and place your caterpillar in it.
7. Water regularly and watch the grass grow.

EGG HEADS

Materials:
- *Potting mix*
- *Egg cups*
- *Grass seed/cress seeds*
- *Soft boiled eggs*
- *Felt tipped pens*
- *Sharp knife, spoon*

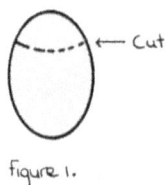

figure 1.

Method:
1. Sit the boiled eggs in the egg cups and carefully cut off the top part of the egg (See Figure 1).
2. Scoop the egg from the shell gently with the spoon.
3. Mix some potting mix with a sprinkle of grass seed.
4. Fill the empty egg shells with the dirt/ grass mix and water regularly. Stand them in a warm spot.

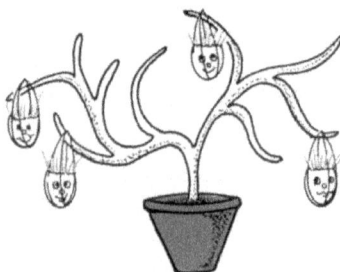

Variations:
- Make the egg heads as above then tape the ends of four pieces of string to the bottom of the egg shell and tie the egg shell in its string basket to the branch of a potted tree.
- Hang several egg heads and you have an interesting egg garden.

AVOCADO TREES

(Take approximately four weeks)

Materials:
- *Avocado stone*
- *Jar*
- *Four tooth picks*
- *Warm water*
- *Flower pot*
- *Soil and pebbles*

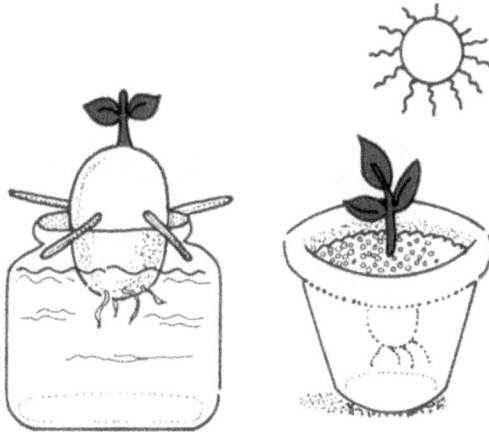

Instructions:
1. Wash the avocado stone carefully.
2. Push the four toothpicks into the stone about one third of the way up from the rounded end.
3. Sit the stone in the jar so the rounded end sits in the warm water.
4. Keep watered until it sprouts some roots.
5. Put the pebbles into the bottom of the flowerpot and the soil on top.
6. Plant the stone in the soil and keep watered and in a sunny place.

BEANS ON BLOTTING PAPER

Materials:
- Broad bean/mung bean or alfalfa seeds (from nurseries or supermarkets)
- Glass jar
- Blotting paper (available from newsagents)
- Water

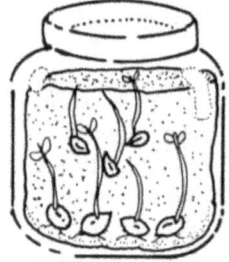

Instructions:
1. Carefully wash and dry the glass jar.
2. Wet the blotting paper and insert it inside the jar going around the inside of the wall in a circle.
3. Drop some bean seeds between the blotting paper and the jar wall.
4. Keep the blotting paper wet and watch the beans grow.

SPROUT JARS

Note: Sprouts are delicious on sandwiches!

Materials:
- A piece of open weave fabric eg. cheesecloth, or a piece of pantyhose.
- Glass jar
- Elastic band
- Water
- Seeds eg broad bean, mung bean or alfalfa

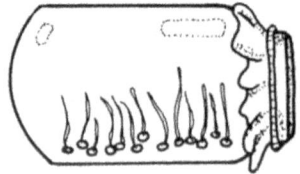

Instructions:
1. Carefully wash and dry the glass jar.
2. Put a handful of the seeds into the jar and cover the top with the cloth. Stretch fabric tightly and secure it with the elastic band.
3. Sit the jar upright and pour water through the cloth lid until the seeds are covered with water.
4. Pour the water back out through the cloth and lay the jar on its side.
5. Leave the jar in a dark place or cover with a tea towel. Repeat watering every day. When sprouts are big enough, eat them!

POTATO HEADS

Materials:
- *Seeds: eg. beans, alfalfa, grass seeds*
- *One large potato*
- *Sharp knife*

Instructions:
1. Carefully use the knife to cut the top off the potato.
2. Make a well inside the potato by cutting away some of the inside of the potato.
3. Insert the seeds into the well and water them.
4. Watch the seeds grow, like hair.

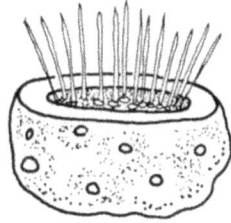

WOOLLY WHEAT

Materials:
- *Polystyrene meat tray*
- *Wad of cotton wool*
- *Water*

Instructions:
1. Wet the wad of cotton wool and line the bottom of the polystyrene tray.
2. Sit the seeds on top of the cotton wool and water again.
3. Water the seeds regularly and watch them grow.

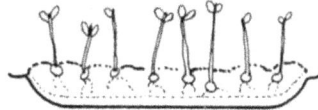

CARROT FERNS

Materials:

- Two toothpicks
- String, two pieces the same length
- Cotton wool
- Saucer
- Water
- Large carrot
- Sharp knife

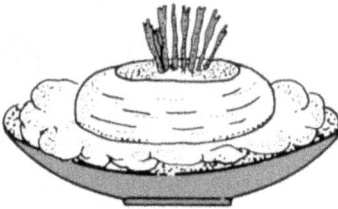

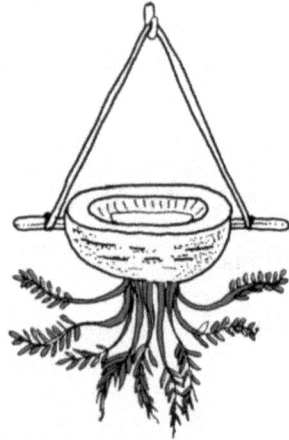

Instructions:

1. Cut a 5 cm section off the large end of the carrot leaving any stalks or shoots attached.
2. Sit the cut end of the carrot top on some moist cotton wool in a saucer. Keep warm and moist until shoots have begun to sprout.
3. Scoop out a bowl shape in the cut end of the carrot top.
4. Push a toothpick through two sides of the upturned carrot top and tie a piece of string to each toothpick.
5. Hang the carrot top upside down in a sunny place and keep the "bowl" filled with water.

PLEASANT PERFUMES

Lavender Bags
Gumnut Fragrance Jar
Pot Pourri
Pomander Balls

LAVENDER BAGS

Materials:

- Lavender flowers (Lavender blooms for about four weeks in January, and it must be picked -then.)
- Needle and thread
- Scissors
- Pretty ribbon
- Coloured nylon netting (available from fabric shops.)

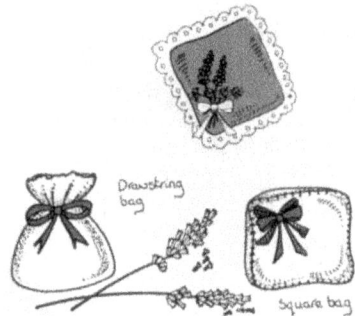

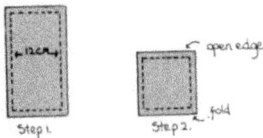

Instructions:

1. Cut a double layer of netting to a size 15 cm x 27 cm. This allows 1.5 cm for a seam around the edge.
2. Fold it in half and sew up two sides to form a bag.
3. Strip the lavender flowers off the stalks and fill the bag with them.
4. Turn the open edge inwards and stitch it up to make a square bag or, for a drawstring bag, make long stitches 1.5 cm from the open edge then pull the thread to bunch the netting together and tie a knot.
5. Decorate your square lavender bag by tying a bow in the ribbon and sewing it to one corner. Tie the ribbon around the neck of your draw-string bag.
- Put lavender bags in your clothes drawers to make your clothes smell sweet.

Variations:

- Sew lace around the edge of the square bag and add a spray of dried flowers.

GUMNUT FRAGRANCE JAR

Materials:
- Gumnuts - assorted sizes (or other large seedpods)
- Eucalyptus oil (from chemists/drugstores or supermarkets)
- A glass jar
- Nylon netting, muslin or other thin cloth
- An elastic band
- Ribbon

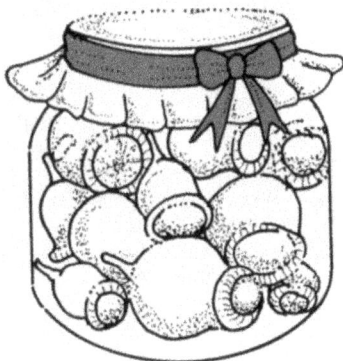

Instructions:
1. Brush the gumnuts clean. They must be thoroughly dry to soak up the eucalyptus oil. Arrange them in the jar.
2. Pour two or three tablespoons of ecualyptus oil over the gumnuts.
3. Cut a circle out of the thin cloth, a lot wider than the top of the jar. Stretch it over the jar, holding it with the elastic band. The edge of the cloth sticks out like a frill.
4. Wrap the ribbon over the elastic band and tie a bow.

- Keep a Gumnut Fragrance Jar on your bathroom shelf to freshen the room. Top it up from time to time with a few extra drops of eucalyptus oil.

POT POURRI

Materials:
- Sweet-smelling petals and leaves
- Orris root powder (available from Chemists)
- Perfume concentrate
- Flywire screen or coarse cheesecloth
- Small jars or baskets or bags made from nylon netting (See "Lavender Bags".)
- Ribbons and dried flowers decoration.

Instructions:
1. Gather the petals of any sweet-smelling flowers that are in full bloom but not past their prime. Petals must be dry when picked. Try to have at least four times as many rose petals as all the others. You can also add the leaves of sweet-smelling herbs such as rosemary.
2. To dry these, place them on the window screen or on the cheese-cloth stretched between two chairs, so that air can circulate around them.
3. When petals and leaves are thoroughly dry, mix them together with a handful of orris root powder and a few drops of perfume concentrate and package them.
- If the potpourri is to go on a shelf you can package it in little jars such as baby-food jars, or tiny baskets, or large sea-shells. Tie ribbons and dried flowers to the basket handles. If it is for a chest of drawers, put it in a nylon netting bag.

POMANDER BALLS

Materials:
- An orange
- A packet of whole cloves
- A meat skewer or a long sharp nail
- Some ribbon

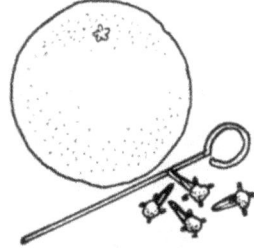

Instructions:
1. Use the sharp end of the skewer to puncture the skin of the orange all over so that you can push cloves into the rind.
2. Stick the cloves as close together as possible, in circles around the orange unti the whole surface is covered.
3. Now push the skewer or nail through the centre of the orange, and tie a ribbon bow to it at each end. Make a long loop of the ribbon to hang it by.
- The orange will shrivel and dry, the oil of its skin blending with the spiciness of the cloves to give a wonderful fragrance.
- Give pomander balls as gifts or hang them in wardrobes and linen cupboards to make clothes smell sweet and spicy.

INDEX

SOME MORE BOOKS IN OUR CHILDRENS' SERIES:

The Parents' Time Off Series:

- Kids' Magical Activities
- Kids' Gardening Activities
- Kids' Cooking Activities
- Kids' Hands-On Craft Activities
- Kids' Fun Craft Activities
- Kids' Creative Craft Activities
- Kids' Games Book 1
- Kids' Games Book 2
- Kids' Nature Activities
- Kids' Holiday Activities

Classic Fairytales from Tolkien's Bookshelf:

- Grimms' Fairytales - Illustrated
- The Red Fairy Book - Illustrated
- The Princess and the Goblin - Illustrated.
- The Story of King Arthur and his Knights - Illustrated

Find out more on our website!

www.leavesofgoldpress.com

THE PARENTS' TIME OFF SERIES

The Parents' Time Off Series — KIDS' MAGICAL ACTIVITIES — Cecilia Egan

The Parents' Time Off Series — KIDS' COOKING ACTIVITIES — Cecilia Egan

The Parents' Time Off Series — KIDS' HANDS-ON CRAFT ACTIVITIES — Cecilia Egan

The Parents' Time Off Series — KIDS' CREATIVE CRAFT ACTIVITIES — Cecilia Egan

The Parents' Time Off Series — KIDS' FUN CRAFT ACTIVITIES — Cecilia Egan

The Parents' Time Off Series — KIDS' GAMES BOOK 1 — Dayton Davis

The Parents' Time Off Series — KIDS' NATURE ACTIVITIES — Cecilia Egan

The Parents' Time Off Series — KIDS' GAMES BOOK 2 — Dayton Davis

The Parents' Time Off Series — KIDS' GARDENING ACTIVITIES — Cecilia Egan

The Parents' Time Off Series — KIDS' HOLIDAY ACTIVITIES — Cecilia Egan

Princess Pam
Fell Into the Jam

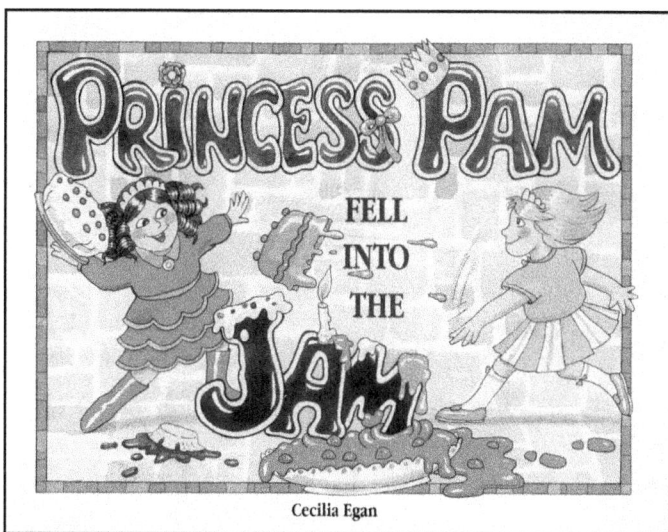

More than a hilarious rhyme, this is a slapstick comedy that causes a riot of laughter when read aloud. Princess Pam and her messy sisters appeal to every child.

The rollicking rhymes, the unconventional story and the lively, detailed pictures combine to make one of the funniest and most original children's books published.

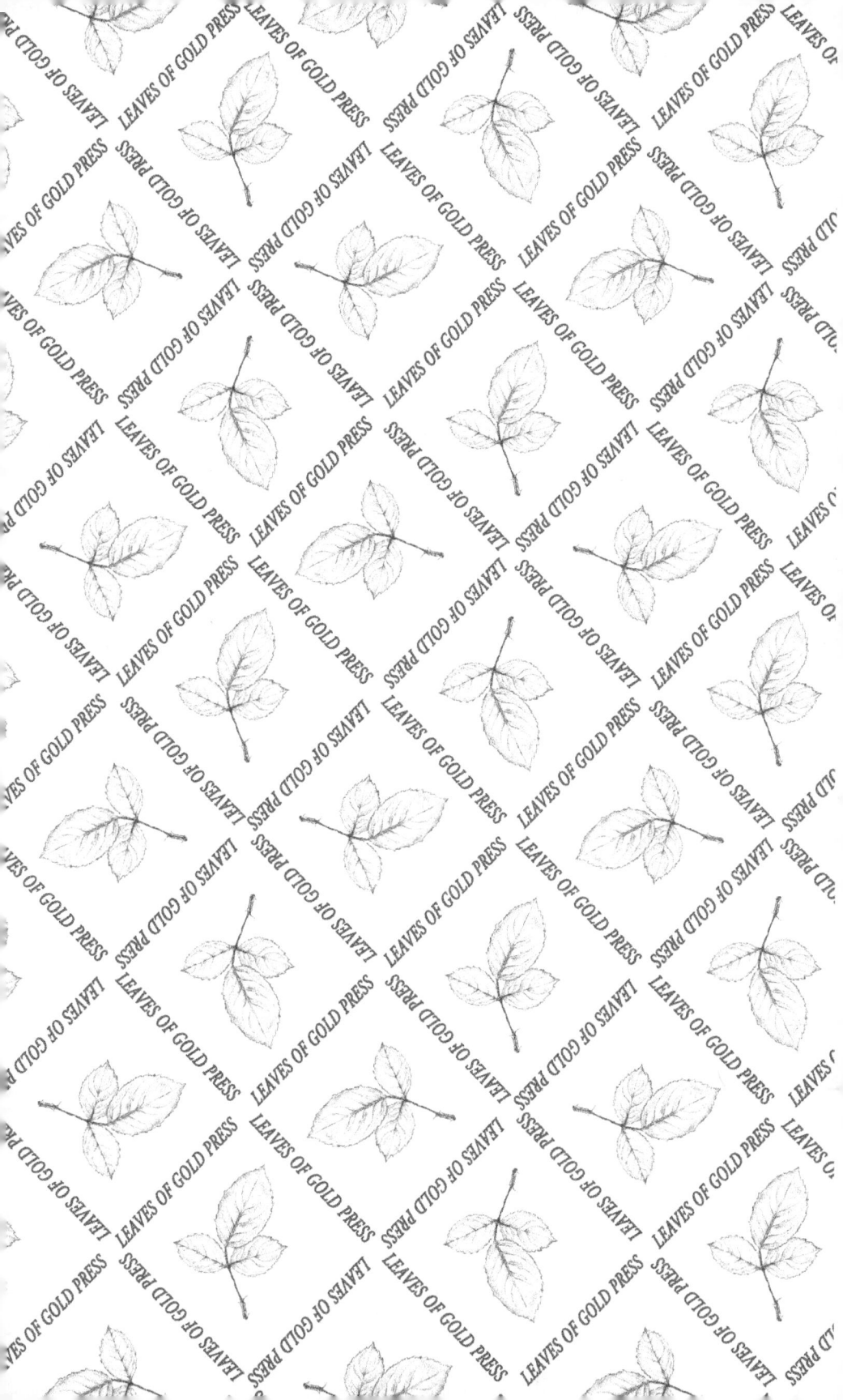

www.ingramcontent.com/pod-product-compliance
Lightning Source LLC
Chambersburg PA
CBHW072210090426
42740CB00012B/2460